Mitch McConnell's Fall at a Washington DC Hotel: All You Need To Know

Copyright

All rights reserved. No part of this publication may be reproduced, distributed, or transmitted in any form or by any means, including photocopying, recording, or other electronic or mechanical methods, without the prior written permission of the publisher, except in the case of brief quotations embodied in critical reviews and certain other noncommercial uses permitted by copyright law.

Table of Content

Chapter 1: Mitch McConnel's Condition After the Fall

After collapsing on Wednesday night, Senate Minority Leader Mitch McConnell is receiving concussion treatment and is anticipated to be in the hospital "for a few days," a spokeswoman said on Thursday.

According to spokesperson David Popp, "The Leader is thankful to the medical staff for their care and to his colleagues for their good wishes. He stated that

McConnell is anticipated to stay in the hospital for monitoring and care.

The 81-year-old senator fell while attending a private dinner at a hotel in Washington.

The meal came after McConnell gave a speech at an event for the Senate Leadership Fund, a super PAC that solicits limitless contributions to back Republican candidates, at the Waldorf Astoria.

During a private meal on Thursday afternoon, senators heard an update on McConnell's health and were informed that he will be in the hospital for several more days, according to some senators. Despite not having talked to McConnell since his fall, Sen. John Barrasso, a member of McConnell's leadership team, stated during the briefing that he believed McConnell was "alive and talking."

He should fully recover, according to Barrasso.

McConnell was reported "up much of the night" in the hospital, but was otherwise in "great spirits," according to Sen. Mitt Romney. McConnell has reportedly been kept up for hours while adhering to a concussion protocol, as was disclosed to the senators.

Several of McConnell's senior lieutenants, including Sen. John Thune, the second-ranking Republican in the Senate, said they hadn't yet talked to him directly as of early Thursday afternoon.

Some senators said that they were not informed of McConnell's scheduled return date but expressed confidence in his well-being. Sen. John Neely Kennedy said, "He's simply rough as a boot.

The president wrote, "Jill and I are wishing Senator McConnell a fast recovery. Senator McConnell and I served in the Senate together for years. We anticipate his return to the Senate floor.

As the party's leader in 2007, McConnell, who was first elected to the Senate in 1985 and is now completing his seventh six-year term. He has served in that capacity for the longest period of anybody, and he has long been one of the most influential elected leaders in Washington.

After stumbling outside of his Louisville home and breaking his shoulder, he had surgery in August 2019. He spent the legislative recess resting at home and attending physical therapy while his recuperation kept him out of the public spotlight for weeks.

The senator, who survived childhood polio, has a history of cardiac problems and had triple bypass surgery in 2003, shortly after being elevated to the No. 2 Republican position in the Senate.

McConnell dismissed questions about his health as media hype when images of his bandaged and bruised hands surfaced in 2020.

On the anniversary of the Ukrainian War, Mitch McConnell urges Americans to "wake up" to the danger posed by Russia.

After a lackluster showing by Republicans in the midterm elections, McConnell overcame the first threat to his leadership by winning reelection as the Senate minority leader in November.

Sen. Rick Scott was soundly beaten by McConnell on a 37-10 vote. Republican infighting highlighted the fact that, despite McConnell's strong conference support, he has lost significant colleagues to retirement. The Senate's average age as of December was 64.

President Biden and the Democrats had a challenging year, and Republican dreams of winning the majority in the Senate were shattered by inept and controversial candidates who had Donald Trump's support.

The gulf between the two men was highlighted by McConnell's criticism of the former president, who he said "proven to be significant" in the result of the midterm elections.

Trump often criticizes McConnell, who claimed that the then-president provoked the assault on the U.S. Capitol on January 6, 2021. Elaine Chao, a former transportation secretary, has been the target of frequent racial jokes and mockery from Trump.

In a call with reporters on Thursday, Trump said, "I disagree with basically everything he does, but I certainly would want him to get well. "I want him to be healthy so he can come back strong."

Last week, McConnell criticized Fox News executives for showing Tucker Carlson's account of the Capitol attack while holding up a letter from Tom Manger, the chief of the U.S. Capitol Police, claiming that Carlson's presentation was "laden with inflammatory and incorrect conclusions."

McConnell told reporters on Tuesday, "I believe it was a mistake for Fox News to portray this in a manner that's absolutely at odds with what our senior law enforcement officer here in the Capitol feels.

The Senate has previously coped with the absence of several legislators less than three months into the term. Sen. Dianne Feinstein, who is 89 years old and the senior senator, just had shingles surgery and is now resting at home.

Over three weeks ago, Sen. John Fetterman admitted himself to the Walter Reed National Military Medical Center with severe depression; a subsequent statement from a staff member said that he "will be returning soon." In recent weeks, some Democratic MPs skipped votes to go to medical appointments or see sick family members.

The Democrats, who have a slim majority, may find it difficult to approve or advance any of Biden's nominations as a result of the absences. This week, Vice President Harris had to cast the deciding vote to confirm two nominees for U.S. district judges.

The difficulties of adjusting to the absences were described earlier this week by Sen. Richard J. Durbin (Ill.), the second-ranking Democrat in the Senate.

"This is the reality I live in," he said. These things will occur, and they do so on both sides of the political line.

Majority Leader Charles E. Schumer said on the Senate floor on Thursday morning that he had contacted McConnell and talked "briefly with his staff to convey my thoughts and best wishes." For "strength and healing for the leader and his family," he said he was praying.

According to Boston University School of Medicine's Robert Cantu, a concussion patient is not routinely hospitalized for more than a few days of observation. The majority get an MRI or CT scan to look for other brain injuries before being sent home to rest.

But, Cantu noted that physicians are probably being very careful with McConnell because of his age, the potential that he has other illnesses or the fact that he may be on meds like blood thinners. He emphasized that he was unaware of McConnell's health or treatment on a personal level.

According to Steven Broglio, director of the University of Michigan's Concussion Institute, following a fall, medical professionals regularly monitor patients for indications of more serious injuries, such as bleeding from the brain.

Even though everyone grows more delicate as they age, Broglio noted the routine works for both younger and older individuals roughly equally.

According to him, there are 22 symptoms of concussion, including headache, weariness, trouble sleeping, attention problems, and brain fog.

According to Broglio, the incidence of concussion is greatest in adults between the ages of mid-teens and mid-twenties, then gradually decreases as people become older and engage in less dangerous activities, and finally slightly increases in later life.

Chapter 2: Future of GOP in doubt after McConnell's hospitalization

Sen. Mitch McConnell, the party's leader, was hospitalized Thursday after stumbling at a private gathering, leaving Senate Republicans shocked and uncertain about his health and the direction of the GOP conference going forward.

Since 2005, McConnell has served as the Senate GOP conference's leader. He has assisted his colleagues through some of the most significant historical events, including the 2008 financial collapse, the

2011 government's impending default, the fiscal cliff of 2012, the two impeachment trials of former President Trump, and January 6, 2021, attack on the Capitol. In January, McConnell became the longest-serving party leader in Senate history.

After leaving a private dinner at the Waldorf Astoria in Washington, McConnell collapsed. He was transported to the hospital in an ambulance and is now receiving concussion treatment.

Just a day before, the 81-year-old Kentucky senator had pushed Democrats to vote against a District of Columbia criminal measure, giving Republicans a significant political triumph. Also, it caused other Republican senators to feel uneasy and concerned about the future.

"Mitch McConnell has my utmost admiration. One Republican senator who spoke about the effects of McConnell's injury on the Senate GOP conference said, "I believe he can lead a very diverse collection of people remarkably.

The senator said, "I wonder who would be our next leader and what type of leader that person would be. Well, I am concerned about it.

"When it comes to projects, he constantly thinks forward. He is considering how the members of his team may work together. I don't believe you find many people with his talent for it, the legislator remarked.

The three candidates seen as McConnell's most probable successors are Senate Republican Conference Chairman John Barrasso, Senate Republican Whip John Thune, and former Senate GOP Whip John Cornyn (Texas).

Yet since McConnell is in a strong position and hasn't made any indication that he plans to step down, there hasn't been any real speculation of a potential contest for Senate GOP leadership among Republican senators.

When Scott attempted to capitalize on Republican dissatisfaction with the results of the 2022 midterm elections by challenging McConnell for the top position, he was soundly rejected by a landslide vote of 37 to 10 by former National Republican Senatorial Committee Chairman Rick Scott.

Scott tweeted on Thursday that he and his wife are keeping the leader and his family "in our thoughts" and wishing him "a quick recovery." Scott and McConnell have been at odds over party policy ever since that election.

Senators were not informed.

Republican senators scrambled the next morning to find out more information about the extent of McConnell's injuries after learning Wednesday night that he had been transported to the hospital after stumbling and falling at a dinner gathering.

The lack of information from McConnell's staff led to wild speculation, and members questioned just how serious the issue was.

Thune and Cornyn, McConnell's senior lieutenants, were hounded for information by reporters in the Capitol's halls before they had a chance to speak with their boss.

Thune just stated, "Don't know a lot yet," on Thursday morning, sporting a sad expression.

To ensure that he addressed his Senate colleagues first, Thune hurried directly to the floor before accepting any more questions. He said that his "thoughts and prayers are with Leader McConnell," as well as "with his family" and "with his staff."

Cornyn was similarly unaware.

I know he's sleeping, but I don't have any further information," he added.

Around noon on Thursday, McConnell's office said that the senator was receiving concussion treatment and will spend a few days being monitored and treated in the hospital.

What precisely took place

A few more details on the disaster emerged during the day.

Earlier that evening, McConnell was at the Waldorf for a reception for the Senate Leadership Fund, a super PAC to which he is connected and which contributed $290 million to the last election.

Many Republican senators attended the reception, which served as a thank-you function for the super PAC's contributors.

Sen. Lisa Murkowski stated, "I believe it was more of a thank you to the folks who had assisted with the fund in the prior election season" (R-Alaska). "Republican colleagues showed up in decent numbers. While I have no idea how many people came, it looked like there were a lot of us.

Afterward, McConnell attended a small, private supper that was "near" to the reception, according to a source familiar with the situation. After that supper, he misstepped and collapsed.

McConnell's lasting influence

Although acknowledging that McConnell's hospitalization raises concerns about the future direction of the Senate GOP conference, the second Republican senator stressed that "it's not the right moment to be talking about [it]."

I hope it's not too bad, the senator said, referring to McConnell's wife, former Transportation Secretary Elaine Chao. "My thoughts and prayers are with Elaine and Mitch," the senator said.

The senator joked, "I haven't discovered anything wonderful about being elderly.

Because McConnell has been such a significant political force in Republican politics for such a long time, his Republican colleagues have come to rely on his capacity to pour enormous sums of money into Senate battleground states and to shield them from the conservative political unrest that has roiled the House GOP conference.

As one of McConnell's closest friends in the Senate and a mainstream and moderate Republican, Sen. Susan Collins of Maine values his leadership because he gives them the freedom to collaborate with Democratic colleagues and engage in the Republican politics they believe are most appropriate for their home states.

Colleagues respect McConnell for his capacity to lead his party out of challenging political circumstances.

One instance of such occurred in the autumn of 2021 when he gathered his leadership group and other supporters to deliver the 11 Republican votes required to clear the way for Democrats to approve legislation to increase the debt ceiling.

Trump and other detractors hammered McConnell severely for the vote, but it eliminated the possibility of a government default.

Additionally, McConnell has previously demonstrated a willingness to intervene in Senate Republican primary politics to clear the way for candidates he thinks will do best in a general election. He adopted this strategy after Republicans missed opportunities to win seats in Delaware, Nevada, Missouri, and Indiana in the 2010 and 2012 elections.

Even the senators who voted to remove him from his leadership position in

November express their appreciation and respect for his fortitude under fire.

He is an experienced crow. Sen. Lindsey Graham remarked, "I'm betting on him...

www.ingramcontent.com/pod-product-compliance
Lightning Source LLC
Chambersburg PA
CBHW061609250726
48657CB00017B/2360